# A Child's Book of Character Building    Book 2

# A Child's Book of Character Building   Book 2

Growing Up
in God's World—
at Home, at School, at Play

*Written and Illustrated by*
**Ron and Rebekah Coriell**

Fleming H. Revell
A Division of Baker Book House Co
Grand Rapids, Michigan 49516

# Contents

# FOREWORD

In a complex, faith-defying world, young Christians need the strength of character to stand up for God, even in the most difficult situations. The first book in this series, *A Child's Book of Character Building*, was designed to help parents guide their children in twelve character traits essential to Christian growth. In a practical yet enjoyable fashion, children ages three through seven were confronted with examples of how they could properly respond to faith situations occurring at home, at school, and at play.

But no twelve character traits alone can encompass every strength the Christian needs, and *A Child's Book of Character Building Number Two* presents twelve more building blocks of the Christian faith. The authors have followed the same successful format, consisting of a definition of each trait, an illustrative Scripture text, and stories from the Bible and other children's lives.

These books are designed for family sharing. When the stories have been read, parents will want to take the opportunity to discuss the concepts described and how they are a part of the Christian life. Children should feel free to respond to these ideas and consider ways they can implement them in daily life.

Through sharing and reaching more deeply into the

Word of God, parents can use *A Child's Book of Character Building Number Two* to help their children develop a vibrant faith that can change their lives. The use of these basics of faith can help even the youngest Christian touch the world for Christ.

THE PUBLISHERS

# Meek

## Patience Without Anger

To speak evil of no man, to be
no brawlers, but gentle, shew-
ing all meekness unto all men.

Titus 3:2

# Meekness in the Bible

"Be sure He does not get away," commanded a guard, as Jesus was roughly pushed along the path leading out of the garden.

The mob made its way to the house of Caiaphas, the high priest. There, in the middle of the night, the Jewish leaders had gathered to put Jesus on trial. He could have disappeared from their midst, as He had done many times before. This time, in meekness, He allowed Himself to be arrested.

False witnesses were brought to lie about things that the Lord had done. Jesus could have proved them wrong. Patiently and without anger, He listened and did not speak out against them. At last, Caiaphas asked Him if He were the Christ, the Son of God. Jesus answered, "Yes."

"He has spoken blasphemy!" shouted the high priest, as he tore his own clothes.

"He is guilty; let Him die!" echoed the other leaders angrily.

Some men spit in His face. He was blindfolded, slapped, and pushed. They mocked Him, laughed, and made fun of Him.

Jesus could have become angry and called upon many angels to rescue Him and slay these wicked men. But our Saviour, in meekness, allowed all this to happen. He knew that He must suffer even worse things and die, in order to pay for the sins of the world.

# Meekness at Home

"Mother, come see the castle I made!" said Mike, excitedly.

Mike almost pulled his mother up the stairs to his room. When they opened the door, there were logs and blocks scattered everywhere. In the center of it all, sat their dog, Sparky!

Mike had spent a long time building his castle. He had diligently put log upon log, until the walls were almost five inches tall. On the back corner there had been a guardhouse with a green roof. A small flag had been stuck in clay so that it would stand on top of the guardhouse.

Mike looked at the scattered pieces. He began to feel very angry. Suddenly, he shouted, "Get out of here!"

Sparky crawled under the bed. With tears in his eyes, Mike buried his head in his mother's lap. "He had no right to wreck the castle," he cried. "It was my castle, not his."

"Mike," his mother said softly, "remember when we got Sparky? You promised you would take care of him and love him. He does not understand about castles. You must learn to be patient and not angry. Jesus was meek. That means when bad things happened to Him, He was patient and did not get upset. Let's pray that the next time you will be strong enough to be like Jesus and be meek."

# Meekness at School

"What is a captain in a spelling bee?" asked Mike's father.

"There are two teams chosen from the class, by the teacher, and each team has a captain," replied Mike. "The captain is always the best speller."

"You sure have worked hard studying your spelling, Mike. You must want to be one of the captains," said Father.

"That's right," responded Mike. "I know I will be one, because I am the best speller in the class."

The next day, Mrs. Nelson, Mike's teacher, chose the players for each team. Mike's name was not called. He was glad, because this meant that he would be chosen as a captain. When his teacher read the names of the captains, he still was not chosen.

"I can't understand this," he whispered to a friend. "Everyone knows that I am the best speller."

Mike almost felt angry. He had worked so diligently to learn his spelling words. Then he remembered that, when he felt like getting angry, he should wait, pray, and see what God wanted him to learn. With determination, Mike controlled his feelings.

Surprisingly, the teacher announced that Mike would be the official referee of the spelling contest. Only the best speller could serve as referee. It was his responsibility to make sure each word was spelled correctly.

Mike understood, now, why he was chosen last. He was glad that he had been meek about the teacher's decision.

# Meekness at Play

"He did it again," Mike murmured beneath his breath. "I told him he could not borrow my bike without asking."

Mike watched through his bedroom window as Dale rode down the sidewalk on a bicycle that looked just like his. Angrily, he thought, *Just wait till I finish my chores. I'll really tell him.*

Hurriedly, he raced to take out the garbage, feed the dog, and rake the yard. As he worked, he became angrier with his friend Dale. At last, he finished. He ran out of the yard to find his bike.

Before he could cross the street, his father called him. "Mike, come see the surprise I have for you."

Reluctantly, Mike turned around and ran to the garage, where his father waited. Opening the door, he was shocked to see his father holding a newly painted bicycle.

"How do you like your bike?" asked Father.

"I thought Dale borrowed it," replied Mike.

"No," responded Father. "He has a new bike just like yours. I thought you would enjoy having a different-looking one. So I painted your bike."

Mike was both thrilled and ashamed. He was glad to have a newly painted bike; but he knew, in his heart, he had been angry and impatient toward Dale. He asked God to forgive him and to give him the strength to be meek.

# Character Development Challenges

## Meekness

1. Ask the child what makes him angry. Discuss how anger can be replaced with meekness, in the situation.
2. Who was the meekest person in Numbers 12?
3. God gives promises to the meek. What are they? Look up Psalms 25:9, Psalms 37:11, and Isaiah 29:19.

# Loyal

## Supporting Someone
## Even When the Going Gets Tough

For we are made partakers of
Christ, if we hold the begin-
ning of our confidence sted-
fast unto the end.

Hebrews 3:14

# Loyalty in the Bible

A lonely figure walked along the barren rocks of the wilderness. Hunger and thirst made His body weary. The Holy Spirit had led Jesus into the wilderness.

The voice of the great tempter, Satan, interrupted His thoughts, "If You are the Son of God, turn these stones into bread."

Jesus replied that the Bible says we must be careful to obey God. It is more important to do what is right than to get bread when we are hungry.

Then Satan took Jesus to a very high part of the Temple, in Jerusalem. He said to Him, "If You are the Son of God, throw Yourself down; the Bible says that the angels will hold You up as You are falling, lest You be killed against a stone."

Jesus would not obey Satan, but was loyal to His heavenly Father. Satan wanted Jesus to obey him and to be his servant. He offered to make Jesus the ruler of the world; but, first, Jesus would have to fall down and worship him.

With authority, Jesus commanded Satan, "Go from Me; for the Bible says to worship the Lord thy God and only serve Him."

When Satan realized that Jesus was loyal to His heavenly Father, he departed from Him.

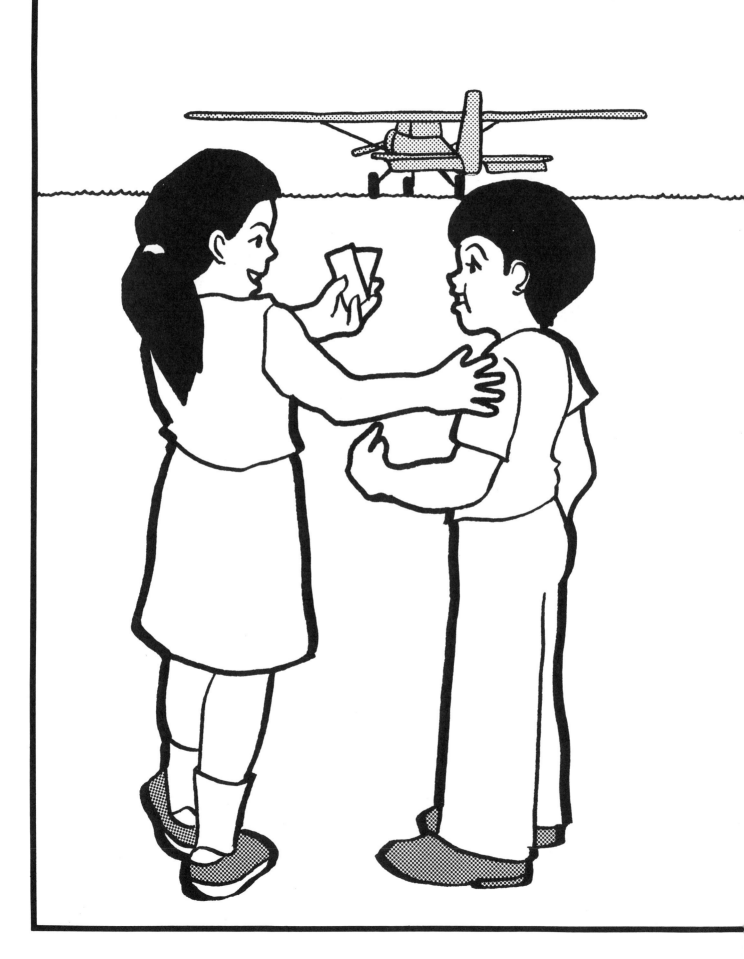

# Loyalty at Home

"Have you ever flown in an airplane?" asked Lilly's younger brother, Bill.

"No, but I sure want to," she answered. "If my vegetables win first place at the county fair, I'll win two tickets for an airplane ride."

"Maybe I can help you," said Bill. "I can weed and water the plants, when they need it."

"Thanks, Bill, that will help," replied Lilly, gratefully.

As the weeks passed, Lilly and her brother worked hard. They planted seeds, sprayed the plants, and pulled weeds. When harvesttime came, Lilly's excitement grew. She knew that her vegetables had a good chance to win.

All Lilly's friends were at the fair the day the judges made their final decision. When they chose Lilly's vegetables as Best in Show, her friends shouted and crowded around to congratulate her.

"Who gets to ride with you in the plane?" asked someone.

"I'm sure it will be her best friend, Mary," said another.

It was a hard decision to make. She had so many special friends with whom to share a ticket. Yet, deep down inside, she knew whom she really wanted to choose.

"Girls, I have made up my mind," she announced. "I am giving the ticket to Bill. I want to be loyal to him, because, without his help, I wouldn't have won."

# Loyalty at School

"I think Mrs. Foster is mean!"

The teacher had just taken two children into the hall, because they were fighting. Many felt that Mrs. Foster was wrong to take both children.

"She should have corrected the guilty one," said one boy.

"Yes," replied another, "the one who did not start the fight should be free."

Lilly could not listen to this kind of talk any longer. Raising her voice, she said, "Stop being so foolish. Mrs. Foster didn't see who started the fight. She took them both, so she could find out what really happened. Mrs. Foster is a good teacher. She loves the Lord and really cares about all of us. I think you are being unfair to her."

Just then, Mrs. Foster brought the two children back from the hall. Both seemed to be friends again.

When the last bell rang, Mrs. Foster asked Lilly to stay, so she could speak to her.

"Lilly," said Mrs. Foster, "someone said that you defended me today. Sometimes being loyal means you have to stand alone on the side of right. This takes courage. God is looking for girls and boys who love Him enough to be loyal and defend Him. Thank you, for being my friend."

# Loyalty at Play

"Here she comes," whispered a girl.

"Let's not say hello as she passes," said another.

Rhoda walked by the group of girls and voiced a friendly hello, but the girls just walked away. As Rhoda sadly turned to go home, one of the girls called out, "We don't play with anyone whose father is a crook!"

Those words hurt so deeply. Rhoda's father was not a Christian. He had been sent to prison for a few months. Now, no one in the neighborhood wanted to be friendly with Rhoda.

Lilly came riding up on her bike. "How about riding to the park with me?" she asked, with a smile.

Frowning, Rhoda answered, "You don't want to be around a crook's daughter, do you?"

"That doesn't make any difference to me," replied Lilly. "Remember, we have to keep praying that your father will come to know Jesus, as you and your mother do. Then your father will be a new person."

"Lilly, why do you want to be loyal to me?" asked Rhoda.

"Because, if friends can't be nice to each other in time of need, then they are not really very good friends," replied Lilly.

Rhoda and Lilly rode to the park together.

# Character Development Challenges

## Loyalty

1. How was David loyal to King Saul? Look up 1 Samuel 24:10 and 1 Samuel 26:8, 9.
2. Help the child memorize Proverbs 17:17, "A friend loveth at all times. . . ."
3. Encourage family or classroom loyalty by not permitting children to ridicule, be sarcastic, or subtly speak against one another.

# Responsible

## Doing What I Know
## I Ought To Do

Moreover it is required in stewards, that a man be found faithful.

1 Corinthians 4:2

# Responsibility in the Bible

As Peter was walking down the street, an important man stopped him. This man was a Temple tax collector. He gathered money from people so the Temple could be run by the priests. The law said people had to pay these taxes.

"Doesn't your Master pay tribute?" asked the collector.

Peter quickly told the man that Jesus *did* pay His taxes. His answer satisfied the man's question, so he left Peter alone.

When Peter returned to the house where Jesus was, his Master already knew what had happened. Jesus also knew what the law said. People would expect Him to be responsible and pay His taxes.

He gave Peter some special instructions: "Go to the sea, put in a hook, and take the fish that first comes up. And when you have opened its mouth, you shall find a piece of money; take it and give it to them for Me and you."

Jesus taught Peter an important lesson. Even the Son of God must be responsible and obey the laws of man.

# Responsibility at Home

"Rita," called her mother, "it's almost time to go shopping. Please pick up the toys in your bedroom."

Rita quickly obeyed her mother and went back to her room. She was surprised when she opened the door. Toys were everywhere! Her younger, twin brothers had taken everything out of the toy box.

*It will take me a long time to pick them up,* she thought. *Mother will think that I'm not being responsible and cleaning up quickly. I had better get right to work and be fast.*

As she hurried to pick up the toys, her brothers watched every move. Then they started to pick up toys, too. Rita thought they only knew how to take toys out. Now they were copying what she was doing. Rita was glad for their help. She was able to get the job done twice as fast.

"Are you ready to go?" asked her mother, as she walked into Rita's room.

"Oh, yes, Mother," replied Rita, with a smile. "I had lots of good help."

"When you are responsible," said her mother, "you teach others to do what they should, too."

# Responsibility at School

"Don't be afraid. Join our game of tag," called a classmate.

Rita didn't know what to do. The bus had delivered children to school early, and the teacher had not arrived at the classroom. Her friends were having a great time, running around the room. Rita knew the school rules said that no one was to run in the building.

*The responsible thing to do,* Rita thought, *is to get a book, sit down, and be quiet. That is what I'll do, even if my friends continue disobeying.*

Taking a book from the reading shelf, Rita went to her seat and began to read. Just then, Mr. Hopper, the principal, appeared in the doorway. Immediately, Rita's friends stopped running.

"Children, into your seats," said Mr. Hopper. "There is to be no running in the classroom." Then he spoke to Rita. "I noticed how responsible you were. I would like you to be in charge of the class until your substitute teacher arrives."

Rita realized that being responsible in little things allowed her to be given greater things to do.

# Responsibility at Play

"Hurry, Rita. Let's see what is inside the package," said her brothers.

Rita tore the paper off the large box. She was so surprised to see a new, shiny, green wagon. After the birthday party, Father and Rita found a place in the garage to store the wagon.

"Rita," said Father, "now that you have a wagon, you must be responsible. When you finish playing with it, you must put it in the garage."

"All right, Father," said Rita. She remembered her father's words for a few days. Then she carelessly left her wagon in the driveway.

The next morning, there was a loud crunch as Rita's father backed the car out of the garage. Rita ran outside to find that her wagon had been bent. She felt very sad. How she wished that she had been responsible and had put her wagon away. That evening, Rita's father repaired the wagon. It was no longer smooth and shiny, but Rita could still ride in it. Now Rita remembers how important it is to be responsible.

# Character Development Challenges

## Responsibility

1.  Invite into the home or classroom someone who acted responsibly in an emergency or a situation. Use his story as a living example of responsibility.
2.  Make a chart with daily chores for the child. Give a star for each responsibility that is completed.
3.  In the Bible, find a person who was responsible. Tell how he pictures this character quality.

# Self-Control

## Doing Something
## Even When I Don't Feel Like It

And every man that striveth
for the mastery is temperate
in all things. . . .

1 Corinthians 9:25

# Self-Control in the Bible

At nine o'clock in the morning, a crowd of angry people brought Jesus to a hill outside the city, to be crucified. Jesus was laid upon a large wooden cross, with His arms and legs outstretched. The soldiers offered Him something to drink, which would deaden the pain. Jesus knew the suffering He would need to endure, but He refused the painkiller. What self-control!

Nails were driven into His hands and feet. Great pain filled His worn body, as Jesus hung before the onlookers.

"Father, forgive them," He said. "They know not what they do."

Before Him stood those whom He had created. Now they were crucifying their Creator. The crowd mocked and jeered Him. Jesus could have called upon thousands of His angels to rescue Him. Yet He knew He must suffer and die for the sins of the world. Thus He continued to allow the torture, even though His body cried out because of the pain. What amazing self-control the Lord possessed.

During the suffering, He spoke only words of mercy and kindness. That day Jesus took the punishment for our sin. Now, our resurrected Saviour offers eternal life to those who believe in Him.

# Self-Control at Home

Thelma was busy helping her parents weed the garden, when she yelled, "Help! Help! A bee is flying around me!"

"Don't move," answered Father. "It won't hurt you, if you sit very still."

Soon, the bee left. Slowly, Thelma moved from plant to plant. Whenever she saw a bee, she jumped and ran to the end of the garden. Her parents noticed that she was not using self-control. Her father called her to his side.

"Thelma, you aren't remembering that I told you to be still when you see a bee."

"I know, Father, and I am sorry. It is because I am afraid of the bees."

Father replied, "Even though the bees are nearby, you must not run. They won't bother you, if you stay calm. Do you remember Philippians 4:13? It says, 'I can do all things through Christ which strengtheneth me.' Jesus can give you the self-control you need."

"All right," she answered. "I will do better this time."

Each time a bee flew past Thelma, she asked God to help her not to be afraid. So Thelma prayed, pulled weeds, and used self-control. Soon all the weeds were pulled.

# Self-Control at School

"I didn't do it," argued Dick.

"Nevertheless, you must suffer along with the rest," said Mrs. Randell, the teacher.

There was a problem in Thelma Johnson's class. Some items had been stolen. Now, Mrs. Randell was making the whole class stay in from recess, until the stolen items were returned. It did not seem fair to Thelma for her teacher to discipline the whole class for the sin of one person. Then she remembered her Sunday-school lesson.

She had studied the story of Achan's sin. God had punished the entire Hebrew nation for one man's sin. That didn't seem fair, either, but Thelma knew that God does not make mistakes. She also knew Mrs. Randell loved and cared for all her students. Yet it was still hard to control herself while sitting inside during recess.

During lunch, some of Thelma's friends spoke to the person they knew had taken the items. He returned them later that afternoon. Mrs. Randell was glad to get them back, but she was even more excited that the class had encouraged the person to return them.

Now, Thelma realized why her teacher had made the entire class suffer. They were forced to help one another to do right. And Thelma was glad that she had the self-control to keep from getting angry with her teacher.

# Self-Control at Play

"Let's go to the museum," said Frank, who was visiting his cousin, Thelma.

"No, let's go to the zoo," said Thelma. "I have been to the museum many times."

"But your cousin has never been there," said her father. "I am sure that he would enjoy seeing all those stuffed animals."

"Live animals are more fun to see than dead ones," pleaded Thelma.

"Yes, but Frank lives near a zoo in San Diego. He has never seen a museum like ours," Father said. "There are old airplanes, a big model-train set, and lots of old cars to see, too. I think it would be best to go to the museum. Let's get ready to go."

Thelma was sad. She did not get her own way. She just knew the museum would be boring. She felt like pouting and staying sad during the whole trip. Yet she also knew that would make four other people very unhappy: Mother, Father, Frank, and her heavenly Father.

It took a lot of self-control to smile, act interested, and try to be happy. As the afternoon passed, it became easier. Near the end of their tour, Thelma was happy that they had gone to the museum.

On the way home, her father whispered in her ear "Thanks, Thelma, for doing something, even though you did not feel like it."

# Character Development Challenges

## Self-Control

1.  Encourage the child to form a good, new habit or break an old, bad one.
2.  Help the child memorize Philippians 4:13.
3.  Have the child draw a picture which illustrates self-control.

# Order

## Everything In Its Place

Let all things be done decently and in order.

1 Corinthians 14:40

# Orderliness in the Bible

Jesus had taught the crowd all day. Everyone was tired and hungry. The disciples suggested that the people be allowed to go into nearby towns and eat.

Jesus said, "Give them something to eat."

The disciples were amazed. Jesus had just told them to feed over five thousand people. Where would they find so much food?

Jesus asked, "How many loaves do you have? Go and see."

Quickly, they searched for food. Soon they came back with five loaves of bread and two fish. They wondered how so little could feed so many.

However, Jesus had a plan. He commanded the multitude to sit down in orderly groups of fifty. This way, it would be easier for them to be served by the twelve disciples. Then Jesus prayed and handed out the food to His helpers. There was enough to feed everyone. It was a miracle!

When everyone was finished eating, all the leftover food was collected. The food filled twelve baskets. Jesus made a big job easy, because He had everything done in an orderly way.

# Orderliness at Home

"Father, come quickly," shouted Gordon, staring out the window.

"What's happening?" asked his father, as he came into the room.

"Look out the window, and you will see," Gordon replied. A spider was carefully weaving a large web. "It's as if he knew we were watching. Look how tiny those threads are. How can he do that?"

"Well, Son," replied Father, "The spider is one of God's most orderly creatures. He made them so that they could build their own houses out of the tiny threads you see. Each thread is made out of silk and is very strong. It comes from inside his body. See how orderly he is in making his web. Each thread must be put in just the right place, so that the wind and rain will not break it. This reminds me, Son. Did you know that children can be orderly, just like spiders?"

"How's that?" asked Gordon.

"Just as spiders have orderly houses, children can have orderly bedrooms. Have you put everything in its place, Son?" asked Father.

"No," he replied, "I guess I haven't. But if a spider can be orderly, so can I." Off Gordon ran, to straighten his room.

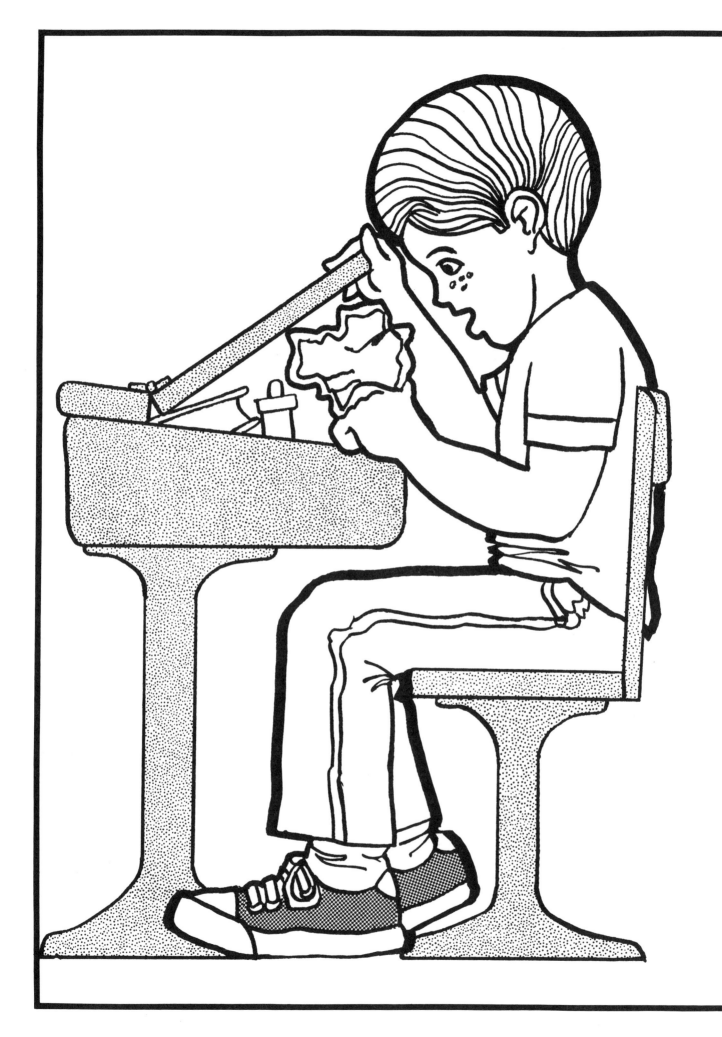

# Orderliness at School

"Gordon, you always have such a messy desk," said a classmate.

Gordon didn't care.

With a look of unconcern, he replied, "I know it. I just don't have time to put everything in its place. Besides, I am busy making this valentine's gift for my mother."

Carefully, Gordon cut red paper into the shape of a heart. Next he cut a larger heart from white paper. He glued the two hearts together so that a little of the white heart showed around the edge of the red heart. Then, he glued a yellow rectangle onto the middle of the hearts, and wrote these words: *Happy Valentine's Day, Mother. I Love You.* How proud he was of the special gift he had made.

Art time ended. Gordon quickly stuffed the valentine into his desk and took out his reading book. By the end of the day, many books had been taken out of and stuffed into his desk.

When it was time to go home, he remembered the gift he had made. He opened his desk, only to discover something terrible. "My present for Mother is all crumpled up!" exclaimed Gordon.

His friend sitting next to him heard his words and said, "That would not have happened if you had kept your desk more orderly."

His friend's words were true. Now he would have to take his mother a wrinkled valentine. But first he would straighten his desk.

# Orderliness at Play

"Thank you, Father! This is what I have always wanted!" Gordon exclaimed. He held up a bright, shiny, new stopwatch.

"Don't lose it, Son. These don't grow on trees," said Father.

During the next few days, Gordon did all kinds of fun things with his watch. He timed how fast birds could fly across his backyard. He discovered that it took over twenty seconds to run around his house.

One day, Gordon became careless about putting his watch in its place. He left it outside, and it disappeared.

*I guess Father found my stopwatch and took it away,* Gordon said to himself, sadly. *This should teach me to be more orderly. Maybe, if I try extra hard to put my things away, he will give it back to me.*

Gordon became more orderly, but the watch was not returned. Then, one day, Father called him. "Look up in that crow's nest," he said.

There, glimmering in the sun, was his shiny watch. Gordon climbed up into the big oak tree in the front yard. Retrieving his watch, he shouted, "The crow must have found my watch in the yard."

"Did you carelessly leave your watch outside?" asked Father.

"Yes, I did," replied Gordon. "Please forgive me for not being orderly. I will try harder to keep all my things in their proper place."

# Character Development Challenges

## Orderliness

1. Orderliness is achieved by having a place for everything. Help the child arrange his desk, closet, or drawer to achieve orderliness.

2. Help the child memorize 1 Corinthians 14:40.

3. Teach the child to set the table, learning the positions of the silverware, plate, and glass or cup. Have the child carry his plate and silverware to the sink after the meal.

# Discern

## Able to See Things As They Really Are

But strong meat belongeth to them that are of full age, even those who by reason of use have their senses exercised to discern both good and evil.

Hebrews 5:14

# Discernment in the Bible

"Stand up and come here," commanded Jesus.

All the people turned to look at the man seated in the back of the synagogue. Slowly, he stood and made his way forward. Ashamed, he tried to hide his paralyzed hand under his cloak. All eyes were fixed on the Teacher and the crippled man before them.

*Now we will see what this Jesus will do,* thought the Pharisees and scribes. *Today is the Sabbath, and our law states that no work must be done. If He heals the man, He is guilty of breaking the law.*

Then Jesus said to them, "I will ask you one thing: Is it lawful on the Sabbath days to do good, or to do evil; to save life, or to destroy it?"

No one answered, not even the wicked religious leaders. Jesus looked at them in grief and in anger. He knew their hearts. He knew their unbelief and hatred.

"Stretch forth your hand," Jesus commanded the crippled man.

From under his cloak, the man put forth a trembling hand. The hand was made instantly whole. The crowd gasped. Quickly, the Pharisees and scribes left the room to plot how to kill Jesus. Then, discerning their intentions, Jesus left the synagogue to continue His ministry.

# Discernment at Home

"Vern," called his mother, "Jason telephoned to ask you to go and play with him tonight. Would you like to go?"

"That sounds great!" Vern said happily. "Jason is fun to play with."

When Vern arrived, Jason invited him into the living room, where the television was turned on. "I am glad you could come, Vern," he said. "I am watching an exciting program."

As the boys watched television, Vern became uneasy. He saw that people dressed immodestly. He heard angry shouts and bad language. The program became filled with violence and unkind actions. Vern knew that the program was not pleasing to God.

Politely, Vern asked if he could be excused to go to the playroom. When Jason finished watching the program, he joined Vern.

"Don't you like to watch television?" asked Jason.

"Some things are all right on television," said Vern. "But since I've become a Christian, I don't enjoy watching that kind of program. The Bible says that our eyes are the light of the body. I want to be sure that thoughts entering my mind are pleasing to God. Anger, violence, bad language, and immodest dress do not please God."

"I never thought about television that way," said Jason. "You are showing me how to be discerning."

# Discernment at School

Vern closed the book. He did not want to fill his mind with things that were not true.

The library book Vern was reading said the earth took millions of years to become what it is today. It further stated that people evolved from animals. This was strange information. Vern knew it could not be true. The Bible says God made the world in only six days. And the first man, Adam, was made from the dust of the ground.

That evening, Vern asked his father about books. "Father, do some books tell the truth and some books lie?" he asked.

"Well, perhaps you might put it that way," he said. "Not *all* books explain things God's way. You must learn to discern which books are telling the truth. These books are best."

Later that evening, Vern had his father take him back to the library. He took the book to the desk to return it.

"Did you enjoy the book, young man?" asked the librarian.

"The pictures were beautiful," replied Vern. "But as I read, I discerned that the book was not telling the truth about how the world began."

"I'm glad that you were so careful with your mind. Sometimes, it is difficult to forget, once we have read a book. Let's go find a book that will please you and the Lord," said the librarian.

# Discernment at Play

"The decision is up to you, Son," cautioned Vern's father. "You must think over each offer carefully before you choose."

Vern had been offered the opportunity to play on two soccer teams in the same league. The Bakersville Rockets were the town's champion team. Most of the team, including the coach, were strangers to Vern. The other team was sponsored by the Christian school he attended. This team was new and needed one more player so it could join the league.

In deep thought, Vern plopped down into a big easy chair to think over his choice. It would be a real honor to play with the Rockets. He was sure the coach was not a Christian, because of the foul language he had used in games last year. On the other hand, his school team would have a Christian coach and players. They really needed Vern to give them enough players to join the league.

The longer he thought, the more he discerned that his best choice would be to support his school team. It would be selfish to join the Rockets because they were champs. Besides, he realized that it would be best to help his school and have Christian companions.

"Father, I have made up my mind to join the school team," Vern said confidently.

"Great, Son," responded Father. "I am glad that you were able to see facts clearly and make up your mind. And I think your choice shows great discernment."

# Character Development Challenges

## Discernment

1. Make a list, with the child, of the things that he should avoid when he views television. Some examples are: violence, anger, dishonesty, foul language, and immodesty.
2. Help the child memorize Hebrews 4:12.
3. Isaiah 7:15 and Romans 12:9 talk about refusing evil and choosing good. Discuss with the child situations in which he should refuse evil and choose good.

# Forgive

## Treating Someone as Though He Never Hurt Me

Forbearing one another, and
forgiving one another, if any
man have a quarrel against
any: even as Christ forgave
you, so also do ye.

Colossians 3:13

# Forgiveness in the Bible

The sight was almost too horrible to view. But angry people were looking on as three men were being painfully crucified on the wooden crosses.

The crowd was interested in the man on the center cross. He was Jesus, who called Himself the Son of God. Most of the people did not believe Him. He had done many kind and helpful things for them. But the religious leaders had lied about Jesus and said that He was a troublemaker. They were jealous of Him, because some people followed His teachings and not theirs.

"If He be the King of Israel, let Him now come down from the cross, and we will follow Him," mocked the rulers (Matthew 27:42).

Others said with a sneer, "He trusted in God; let Him deliver Him now, if He will have Him: for He said, I am the Son of God" (Matthew 27:43).

Even one of the two thieves who were crucified on each side of Jesus said unkind words about Him. No one seemed to care about Jesus.

Was Jesus angry with these cruel people? No, He forgave them, because He loved them. As He hung in pain He prayed, "Father, forgive them; for they know not what they do" (Luke 23:34).

*This story is found in Matthew 27:35-51; Luke 23:33- 38.*

# Forgiveness at Home

"I just couldn't wait to tell Father about the birthday present you bought him," explained Robby to his older brother, Dennis.

"But you promised not to tell," replied Dennis. "For weeks I've planned to surprise Father with a new tie."

Robby did not understand how deeply he had hurt his brother's feelings. Dennis slowly walked away. Noticing the sad expression on his face, Mother followed Dennis into his room.

"Do you love your brother?" asked Mother.

Dennis was surprised at her question. "Of course I do," he replied.

"I know you feel that he has not treated you kindly," comforted Mother. "I also know that Jesus was treated unkindly by the people who crucified Him. Yet He showed His love for them by asking His Father to forgive them. A good way in which you could show your love for your brother would be to forgive him. Treat him as if he never hurt you. I know you do not feel like it. But do it anyway, because it is the right thing to do."

Dennis stayed in his room for a while. Then he came out smiling. Dennis did love his brother, and he showed it by forgiving him.

# Forgiveness at School

The class was only making one clay project this year. Dennis was proud of his clay turtle, because it looked so real. Someone told him it was the most carefully made project in the class.

Clay has to dry completely before it can be baked hard. Each of the students carefully placed his project on a shelf, so it could dry for a few days. Every day Dennis inspected his turtle to see if it was dry. On Wednesday he discovered that it was broken.

"Who broke my turtle?" Dennis shouted.

Carma stammered, "I — I did, and I — I'm so sorry. I picked it up to look at it, and it slipped out of my hand."

Dennis gave her an angry look and sat down in his chair, in a huff. His teacher talked to him about his attitude: "Dennis, being angry will not put your turtle back together. Being angry at Carma is a way of hurting her. She is sorry that she broke your project. She really needs you to forgive her, so that she will feel better. When you do, you will feel better, too."

Later that day, Dennis took his teacher's advice. He forgave Carma, and they were friends again. Both felt better when Dennis forgave Carma.

# Forgiveness at Play

It was hard to stand on the sidelines and watch. Dennis had hoped to play in the game. His coach had promised that he could be a starter; but at the last moment the new boy had arrived, and the coach had allowed him to take Dennis's place.

*It sure is unfair for the coach not to let me play,* thought Dennis. *I think I had better pray about this, before I get angry.*

Silently, Dennis prayed and asked God to help him. He forgave his coach. He told the Lord that he was even willing to sit out the whole game if that was what was best for the team.

The game ended, and Dennis did not get to play. He felt sad, but he was happy that his team had won. He congratulated everyone, even the coach.

After everyone had left, the coach called to Dennis, "Dennis, I want to tell you something. I know I did not keep my word and let you play. I was wrong. You did not even get angry. That is the kind of player we need. Tomorrow, you will play the whole game."

As Dennis went home he was glad that he had learned how to be forgiving.

# Character Development Challenges

## Forgiveness

1. Encourage the child to do good to someone whom he needs to forgive (Matthew 5:44).
2. Each time a child comes to report a wrongdoing, ask him if he has forgiven the person who has hurt him. If he has not, help him to pray to God, forgiving the person who has harmed him.
3. When a child is unwilling to forgive, ask him to recall a situation in which he needed forgiveness from God and encourage the child to forgive as he has been forgiven.

# Fair

## Treating Others Equally

. . . observe these things
without preferring one before
another, doing nothing by
partiality.

1 Timothy 5:21

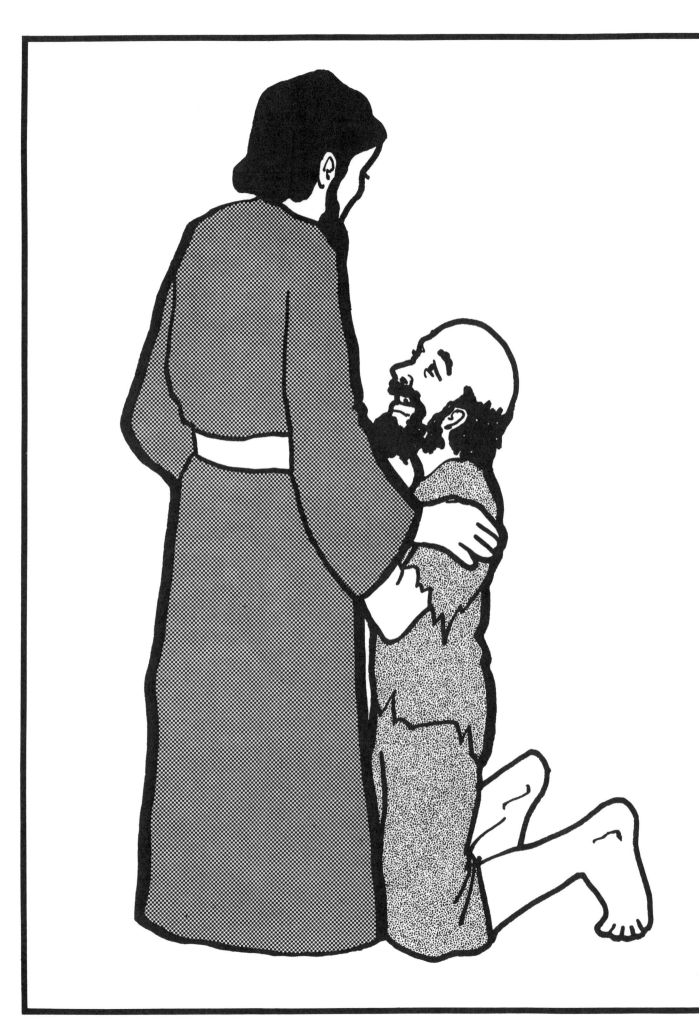

# Fairness in the Bible

The ten men were careful not to let anyone come near them. As people approached, they would call out, "Unclean, unclean!" These men were lepers.

One day, Jesus entered the village where the men were. Although they stood far away, the lepers recognized Him. They cried out, "Jesus, Master, have mercy on us!" (Luke 17:13).

Jesus paused to look at the men. Their clothes looked ragged. Their bodies were thin, and they were covered with sores. Nine of the men were Jews, and one was a Samaritan. Most Jews hated Samaritans. They tried not to talk to them. They would not even walk through the land of Samaria. Would Jesus heal only the nine Jews? Or would he treat all ten lepers equally?

Jesus replied, "Go show yourselves unto the priests."

As the ten turned to go, they discovered that they were healed. The Samaritan shouted glory to God. Then he came back to Jesus and fell at His feet. Over and over again, he thanked Him.

Jesus was fair to the ten lepers. He healed them all, even though one was a Samaritan.

*This story is found in Luke 17:11-19.*

# Fairness at Home

Amy squealed with excitement when she heard that her friend, Donna, was coming to spend the night. But Amy's younger sister, Tammy, just frowned.

"It will be wonderful," said Amy. "We will practice our spelling words together, ride bicycles, listen to records, and play some games."

Tammy said nothing. She just looked at the floor. Amy talked about all that she and her friend would do together.

Noticing that her sister did not seem to be happy for her, Amy asked, "What is the matter? Aren't you happy for me, Tammy?"

Tammy paused. The words didn't want to come out. At last she grumbled, "You are not being fair. All afternoon and evening you are going to play with Donna. She is my friend, too. You talk as if you do not want me to play with you and Donna."

Amy felt guilty about her words. She was talking as if Donna were her only playmate. She did want her sister to join them in the fun-filled day.

"I'm sorry, Tammy," said Amy. "Forgive me for not treating you fairly. You will always be my best friend. I want us both to have a good time with our guest tomorrow."

# Fairness at School

Amy sat alone on the school steps. All her friends were busy talking to Cindy, the new girl who had come to school that day. She was dressed so nicely. Some of the boys forgot to play kickball; they were too busy trying to get the new girl's attention.

"Recess is no fun today," muttered Amy. "I wish Cindy had not come. I'm not going to fuss over her, like those kids are doing!"

Mr. Whiston, the playground supervisor, walked up to Amy. "You look lonely," he said.

"I am," responded Amy.

"Don't you want to join the others?" he questioned.

"No," she answered. "I'm not going to treat that new girl specially. I don't even like her."

"Then you are not being fair to her," he said. "If you ignore her, you are treating her *very* specially. And you will not get to know her and find out if she would be a nice friend. Why not be fair and give her a chance?"

Mr. Whiston's words made sense. The other children did look as if they were having fun with Cindy.

*All right, I'll be fair and treat Cindy just like all my friends,* thought Amy as she ran over to join the group.

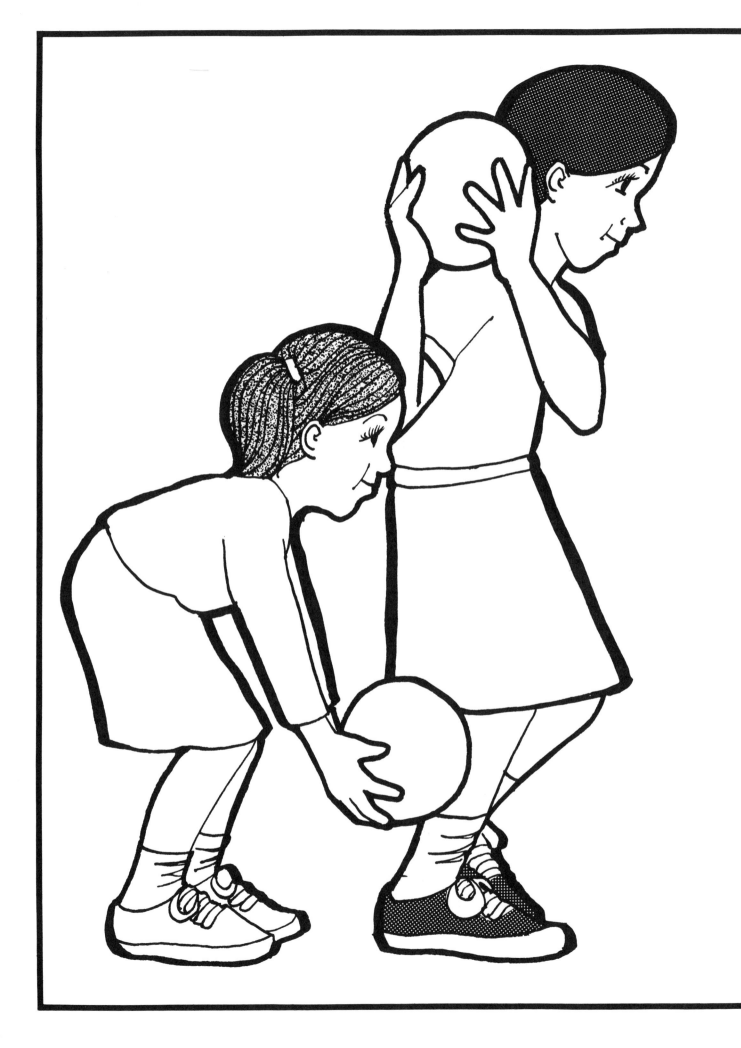

# Fairness at Play

Dodge ball is one of Amy's favorite games. She plays it every Saturday with her friends at the park. One day she was especially having fun, because she was winning almost all the games. She could throw and catch the ball very well.

As they played, Amy noticed that a little friend named Trudy always seemed to be the first girl out. She was not a fast runner, and she could not throw or catch the ball well. The older girls always threw the ball at her first.

"That is so unfair," said Amy to a friend on her team. "She must not have very much fun being hit first."

"But how can we help that?" asked her friend.

"I have an idea," said Amy.

She whispered in her teammate's ear. Then they picked up the balls and began the game. They stayed near Trudy. The older girls on the other team didn't dare hit Trudy now. They were afraid Amy would get them out. Trudy had so much fun in that game. She even got some other girls out. Amy's heart was glad because now Trudy was being treated more fairly.

# Character Development Challenges

## Fairness

1. Whenever an item is divided among children, allow one child to cut or divide it. Give the first choice to the other children.
2. The child should memorize Proverbs 15:3, to remind him that God is watching to see if he is fair.
3. Explain Christ's words, "So the last shall be first, and the first last . . ." (Matthew 20:16). Use this verse as a motivation for the child to put others before himself.

# Tolerant

## Accepting Others, Even if They Are Different

My brethren, have not the faith
of our Lord Jesus Christ, the
Lord of glory, with respect of
persons.

James 2:1

# Tolerance in the Bible

Jesus was often invited into people's homes for dinner. He would meet many different families and would teach them about God. On one occasion He was asked into the home of two sisters who were as different as night and day.

Martha had a servant's spirit and was always looking for a way to help others. With great joy she began to collect the things she would need to cook a delicious meal for Jesus.

On the other hand, her sister, Mary, was a learner. She knew that Jesus was a great teacher. She was excited about hearing Him speak to her in person. Cooking and serving dinner were the furthest things from her mind. Eagerly she sat near Jesus and began to listen as He talked.

Martha became troubled. She said, "Lord, dost Thou not care that my sister hath left me to serve alone? Bid her, therefore, that she help me" (Luke 10:40).

Jesus told her in a kind way not to be worried about Mary. She had wisely chosen to listen to His teaching.

Jesus knew that Martha wanted to be a helper. Therefore, He was tolerant of her complaint and did not get angry. He accepted her even though she was different from her sister, Mary.

*This story is found in Luke 10:38-42.*

# Tolerance at Home

Pamela waited eagerly for mother to arrive home with Teresa, the new baby. She had prayed a long time for a new sister. Now, at last, she would have one.

However, all her dreams and hopes were shattered when her mother brought the baby home. She was a different kind of baby. Pamela's mother told her that her new sister had been born with a withered arm and that it would never grow to be normal. She would never be able to play baseball or sew.

Pamela was really ashamed of Teresa. She did not like to look at her or even want to show her to her friends.

Noticing Pamela's wrong attitude, her mother encouraged her, "Pamela, God made Teresa just the way she is. God never makes a mistake. He must have a special purpose for her life. We don't undertand it now, but maybe we will later. I hope you will be more tolerant of her and learn to love her as well."

As Pamela watched her parents lovingly take care of her new sister and daily thank God for her, Pam's attitude toward her began to change. Soon she was asking to help hold, feed, and rock her.

Pamela was learning to accept Teresa, even though she was different; and, as a result, God helped her to develop a special love for her new baby sister.

# Tolerance at School

"Students, I would like you to meet a new classmate," announced Mrs. Baker, the teacher. "Her name is Susie Wong and she is from China. I'm sure you will want to get to know her."

As Susie took her seat some of Pamela's friends giggled. The new girl did not hear them.

During recess, Pamela asked her friends what was so funny.

"She's not like us," said one friend. "She looks different and she talks funny."

"That is no reason to laugh at her," responded Pamela.

"Well, if you want to be her friend, go ahead," they said. "We don't want to be friends with a girl who looks and talks differently."

Pamela was sorry that her friends were not more tolerant. She did not let this stop her from becoming friends with the new girl.

Pamela soon found that Susie was very friendly and very talented. She taught Pamela how to paint pretty flowers with watercolors. She also taught her some Chinese words.

Being tolerant helped Pamela to understand and enjoy a new friend.

# Tolerance at Play

Pamela was disappointed. Her mother told her that they would have to baby-sit a neighbor two afternoons a week, while her parents were at work. The neighbor, Carol Connors, was handicapped with polio. She had to use crutches in order to walk.

"Mother, how can we have fun together if she cannot ride a bike, swim, or run?" asked Pamela.

"You will just have to find other things to do," replied Mother.

Pamela accepted her mother's words and decided to try to be tolerant of her new playmate.

On Tuesday, Pamela spent her first afternoon with Carol. Time passed very slowly. The girls didn't know what to do together.

Finally, Carol said, "Let me show you how to play my harmonica. I'm taking lessons now."

Pamela's parents could not afford music lessons. However, Carol was willing to teach Pamela everything that she was learning. An inexpensive harmonica was bought for Pamela. Before long, she and Carol could play duets.

"Carol is so much fun," Pamela told her mother one day, after Carol had gone home. "At first it wasn't easy for me to accept playing with a crippled friend."

"Yes," replied Mother. "But God will always help us to be tolerant, if we are willing to try."

# Character Development Challenges

## Tolerance

1. The child should recognize three good characteristics in the life of a person whom he needs to tolerate.
2. Invite into the home or classroom someone from a different country, who can share different customs and life-styles.
3. Acquaint the child with the life story of the blind hymn writer Fanny Crosby. Help him see that someone with a physical handicap has the same emotions and desires that the child experiences.

# Initiate

## Making the First Move
## Without Being Asked

Go to the ant, thou sluggard;
consider her ways, and be wise:
Which having no guide, overseer,
or ruler, Provideth her meat in
the summer and gathereth her food
in the harvest.

Proverbs 6:6-8

# Initiative in the Bible

It was a hot midday when Jesus sat down at a well to rest from His walk. At the same time, a Samaritan woman came to the well to draw water.

In the land where Jesus lived, the Jews did not like Samaritans. They did not even like to talk to them. Jesus was a Jew, yet He took the initiative and spoke to the woman at the well. Because He is God, He knew that she needed to ask Him to be her Saviour.

She was surprised. She never expected a Jewish man to speak to her first. But, the more they talked, the more she realized that He was not an ordinary man.

She said, "I know that Messiah cometh, who is called Christ: when He is come, He will tell us all things" (John 4:25).

Jesus replied, "I who speak unto thee am He" (John 4:26).

The initiative of Jesus convinced this woman that He was no ordinary man. She later brought others to hear His teaching.

*This story is found in John 4:5-30.*

# Initiative at Home

Adam pulled the covers over his head as Father's alarm clock rang. He and his family had been up late the night before and everyone was still sleepy. The alarm ran down without being shut off. One-half hour later, with one eye open, Adam looked at his own clock.

"It is late!" he shouted. "Mother, Father, we will be late for church! We have to get up now!"

Adam put on his robe and set out his Sunday clothes. He wanted to help the family get to church on time.

*I know what I can do*, he thought. *I will make my bed. Then I will surprise Mother and Father by making their bed, too. They will not have time to do it themselves.*

It took only minutes to complete these jobs. Then Adam washed his face, dressed, and came downstairs for breakfast.

Father had already noticed his son's kind helpfulness. "Mother," said Father approvingly, "we have a son who shows initiative. He made all the beds without even being asked. Thank you, Son. It will help us not to be late for church."

# Initiative at School

Adam was hanging up his coat in the classroom when he noticed a book lying on the floor. It didn't look like any of the books used in his room. A paper clip was attached to the cover of the book. Adam opened the book and found a card, which read: "Whoever finds this lost book, please return it to the principal's office."

Adam tucked the book under his arm and went to his seat. He put it in his desk and took out his math book.

The school day was filled with many exciting activities. But all day long, Adam wondered about the note attached to the "lost" book.

When the school day ended, Adam gathered his homework and remembered to put the "lost" book in his schoolbag. Then he stopped by the principal's office.

Mr. King, the principal, greeted Adam with a smile. "I see you have found one of my lost books. Thank you for returning it."

"You mean you lost more than one book?" asked Adam.

"Oh, yes," replied Mr. King. "I purposely lost five books. I wanted to see who would take the initiative to return them to me. In return, I have a special award for you."

Adam was glad he had taken the extra effort to show initiative.

# Initiative at Play

Adam Randall's backyard had the most beautiful flower garden in the neighborhood. His grandpa spent many hours lovingly caring for these plants. But Adam didn't pay much attention. He liked baseball better than flowers.

One sunny afternoon, while Adam and his friends were playing ball, Jeff, his little brother, began to pick Grandpa's flowers. Grandpa was lying on the porch swing asleep. Adam saw what his brother was doing, but he just didn't care to stop playing ball long enough to tell someone or to stop Jeff.

Later, Grandpa woke up and saw what Jeff was doing.

"Adam," he called, "didn't you see Jeff picking my flowers?"

"Yes, Grandpa," said Adam as he ran to him, "but I was too busy playing ball. I'm sorry it happened."

Grandpa looked unhappy. "Saying you are sorry doesn't put back my flowers. Jeff is too young to understand. You must use initiative. If you see him doing wrong, don't wait. Help him to do what is right."

Grandpa grew more flowers, and Jeff learned not to pick them. But, most important, Adam learned that when he knows how to do good, he must take the initiative and do it without being asked.

# Character Development Challenges

## Initiative

1. The child should think of three ways to help his father during the week and do the tasks without telling anyone.
2. The child should memorize James 4:17, to encourage initiative.
3. The child should ask a grandparent or older person how he showed initiative as a child.

# Love

## Unselfishly Meeting Another's Need

This is my commandment, That
ye love one another, as I have
loved you.

John 15:12

# Love in the Bible

One day, while Jesus walked along a road, a group of people came to Him. They brought a man who was deaf and who had trouble speaking.

"Please, heal our friend," they begged Jesus.

As He looked at this man, Jesus loved him. He wanted to heal him. Meeting someone's need is the best way to show that you love him.

Jesus led the man a little distance from his friends. There He did a strange thing. Jesus put His fingers in the deaf man's ears. Then He spit and touched the man's tongue.

Looking up to heaven, He sighed and said, "Be opened" (Mark 7:34).

Immediately, the man could hear and could talk plainly. It was a miracle!

Jesus could have asked the man to tell everyone what a great healer He was. He would have gained much fame. However, Jesus healed the man because He loved him, not because He wanted to be famous. So He told the man not to tell anyone what had happened.

Jesus showed the man how truly He loved him. He healed him without selfishly expecting any reward.

*This story is found in Mark 7:31-36.*

# Love at Home

When his father was away from home on business trips, Roy missed him very much. This time, Roy could not wait for his father to return. He wanted to show him his report card. There was a great improvement in Roy's grades.

Davey, Roy's little brother, also missed Father. He was too young to understand why Father did not come home each night. After a few days, Davey became very lonely. He would ask Mother over and over again, "When will Father come home?"

Both boys ran to the picture window as they heard the familiar sound of Father's car in the driveway.

"Now I can show my report card to Father," Roy told his brother.

Davey yelled for joy, "Father, Father!"

Roy remembered how lonely his brother had been all week; he realized that Davey needed to see Father much more than he did.

*Meeting someone's need is a good way to show that you love them*, Roy reminded himself. *I love my brother more than any friend I have. So I'll let him see Father first.*

What a joy it was for Roy to watch Davey throw himself into Father's arms. Love was meeting his brother's need.

# Love at School

The wind blew against the school bus. The bus shook. It was a windy spring day. As the bus rolled to a stop Roy and his friend, Terry, gathered their books and papers.

"Hold on tight to your papers and things," said Terry. "That wind is really strong."

Roy agreed and held his books tightly against his chest as he stepped off the bus. The wind was blowing so hard that he could hardly breathe. Finally he and Terry turned around and walked backwards.

They were almost inside the building when Terry fell.

"Roy, my papers!" yelled Terry as his papers and books slipped out of his hands.

Roy set his things down and immediately ran after Terry's papers and books. The books didn't go far, but the papers blew across the school yard, and pressed against a fence. There Roy and his friend were able to save them all.

"Thanks, Roy," said Terry. "I couldn't have saved my papers without your help."

"I was glad to do it," said Roy. "The Bible says we are to love our neighbors. To love is to meet someone's need, and you needed help."

# Love at Play

Roy could not wait to get home, change his clothes, and join his friends playing baseball. He rushed up the stairs, taking off his shirt and pants as he went. In less than five minutes, he had changed into his play clothes.

"Come on, Roy," a friend outside shouted. "The game is almost ready to start."

This made Roy rush even more. Down the stairs he hurried and out the door. He had almost run out of the backyard when he stopped. Looking down at his feet, he realized that he had forgotten to change his shoes. He was still wearing his good school shoes.

*Oh, what shall I do?* he thought. *If I go back to change my shoes, I'll be late for the game. But if I don't change, I'll be disobeying Mother.*

It was a hard decision for Roy to make. He thought it over before he decided. Then he went back to his room for his play shoes.

"What made you change shoes?" asked Mother, who had watched Roy trying to decide what to do.

"Well, I know you need and want a son who will obey you," said Roy. "And I love you more than baseball."

# Character Development Challenges

## Love

1. The child should memorize Mark 12:30, 31. Have him use these motions when reciting the verse:

   Heart — draw a heart in the air
   Soul — point to his chest
   Mind — point to his head
   Strength — flex his arm muscles
   Neighbor — point to others
   Thyself — point to himself

2. Using Psalms 116:1 as an example, have the child write a psalm stating why he loves God: "I love the Lord because _____."

3. The child should find a way to use his hands and his feet to show love, and his tongue to speak love to someone.

# Generosity

## Sharing What I Have
## With a Happy Spirit

Every man according as he purposeth
in his heart, so let him give; not
grudgingly, or of necessity: for
God loveth a cheerful giver.

2 Corinthians 9:7

# Generosity in the Bible

Jesus was a poor man. He did not own a house, a camel, or expensive clothes. He did not receive pay from working at a job. It would seem that Jesus had nothing to give to anyone else. One cannot share what he does not have.

However, Jesus was a very generous person. He shared again and again with people in need. He always did it with a happy spirit.

Jesus shared His healing power by helping Peter's mother-in-law get well. He once shared three days of His time to teach thousands of people on a mountain. Though tired from walking many miles, He still witnessed to a Samaritan woman by a well. He stopped to hear the cries of blind Bartimaeus and then healed him. Jesus took time to bless young children who were brought to Him by their mothers. He shared food and shelter with the disciples whom He had trained for three years. While at prayer one night, Jesus realized that the disciples were in danger as they sailed across a stormy lake. He quickly went to rescue them.

Jesus was indeed generous. Though He was poor, He did have wisdom, healing power, time, and love. These He shared freely.

# Generosity at Home

The Decker family enjoyed having missionaries as guests in their home. The missionaries would often come to their church to speak, and Mr. Decker would invite them home.

However, Sheri did not enjoy missionaries as much as the rest of the family. She always had to give up her room, so they could sleep in her large double bed.

"Mother, why can't missionaries stay somewhere else next time," pleaded Sheri. "I always have to give up my bed."

Mrs. Decker looked surprised and disappointed. "I'm sorry you feel that way. It is a special privilege to have these people in our home. Some of our missionary friends influenced your older sister, Laura, to serve the Lord in Africa. When we entertain them, they tell us interesting stories that you love to hear. And we discover what they need, so that we can pray for them."

Sheri paused to think about her mother's words.

"I had not thought of it that way," she said. "I feel better about giving up my room."

"I'm so glad," responded Mrs. Decker with a smile. "You are being generous when you share what you have with others, with a happy spirit."

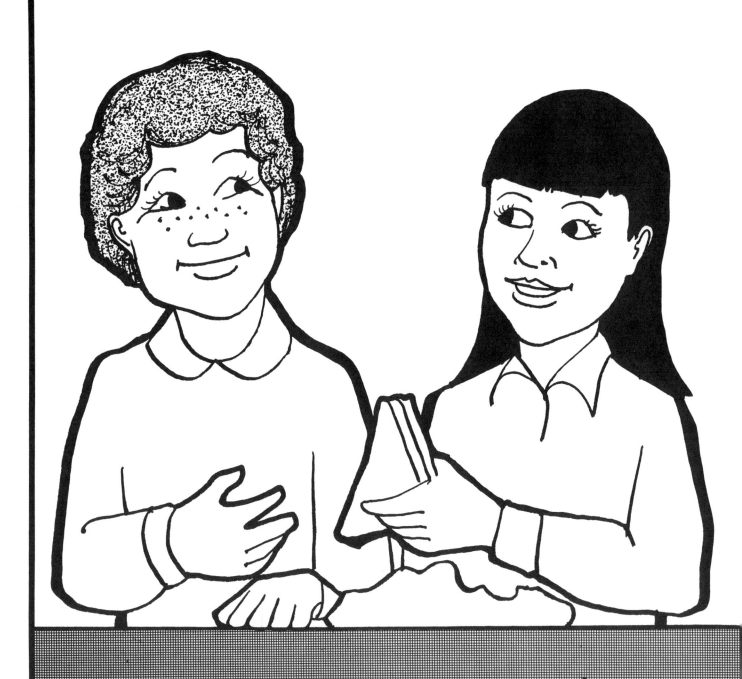

# Generosity at School

Sheri's favorite lunch is a peanut-butter-and-banana sandwich, potato chips, and a carton of milk. She looked forward to Fridays with excitement. This was the only day her mother packed her favorite meal.

When the lunch bell rang, Sheri quickly put away her books and got out her lunch box. As she unwrapped her sandwich, she noticed that her friend Jill had a sad look on her face.

"What is the matter? Don't you like what your mother gave you to eat?" asked Sheri.

"I am sad because I forgot my lunch," Jill answered.

Sheri felt sorry for her friend. She thought Jill must be very hungry. It would be a long time until school was over. Sheri looked at her peanut-butter-and-banana sandwich.

"Here," she said, "you can eat half of my sandwich. And I have some potato chips to share, too."

Jill's face brightened. She eagerly accepted her friend's generosity.

Although Sheri ate only one-half of her favorite lunch that Friday, it was worth it. It made her happy to meet someone else's need.

# Generosity at Play

The new bicycle was bright in the sunlight. Sheri waited eagerly to ride it as her father finished putting air in the tires.

"Hurry, Father," she said. "I can't wait to ride the bike."

Mr. Decker was glad that Sheri was happy with her birthday bike. At last he finished, and Sheri jumped on and pushed up the kickstand.

"Here I go!" she called as she rode down the sidewalk.

Before Sheri had passed two houses, a friend ran up to see her new bicycle. Father watched the girls talk excitedly for a while. Then he saw Sheri get off and allow her friend to ride the bike. Up and down the sidewalk the friend rode while Sheri watched. Father paid close attention to see if Sheri minded that her friend rode so long.

Later, Mr. Decker spoke to Sheri. "I want to tell you how happy I am that you are a generous girl. I watched you as you let someone else ride your new bike. You shared with a happy spirit."

# Character Development Challenges

## Generosity

1. Start a tradition in your home by using your child's birthday as an opportunity for him to give a present to his birthday guests, brothers, or sisters.
2. The child should compile a list of Bible characters who were givers (generous) and takers (selfish).
3. Have the child list ways in which he could be generous:

    I will give my time to help _____ .

    I will let _____ use my favorite toy.

    I will share my _____ with _____ .

    I will cheerfully give _____ to the Lord.